NeVER MIN

B*LL*CKS

A PHOTOGRAPHIC RECORD OF

THE SEX PISTOLS

96 PAGES OF PHOTOS INCLUDING FOR THE
FIRST TIME 16 PAGES OF COLOUR PICTURES
BY DENNIS MORRIS

OMNIBUS PRESS
LONDON · NEW YORK · SYDNEY

Dennis Morris Publications

Foreword

"I got involved with the Pistols purely by chance. At that time I was doing a lot of photography for Virgin Records who had just signed the band. Tessa Watts from Virgin approached me to see if I would be interested in doing some work with them and my answer, of course, was yes. She told me my name would be added to the list of photographers she was making for Malcolm McLaren. Two days later I got a call. I was the chosen one.

"It seemed John knew my work because he was a reggae fan. When John and I first met it was as if we already knew each other; in fact, we later found out we used to go to the same clubs. Having spent time working with reggae musicians whose lyrical content was very potent, I now found myself working with a band who had untold energy and lyrical content equal to all the great reggae musicians. It was a perfect combination.

"This is a photographic record of one of <u>the</u> most influential bands ever to have come out of Britain. These pictures were taken on their 'secret' tour. Having been banned from playing in many parts of Britain, they found themselves playing shows in small clubs that had been fixed up at the last moment. Under the most ridiculous of circumstances they played in front of hysterical audiences, sometimes never even playing a full set before chaos broke loose.

"Needless to say, the conditions in which the pictures were taken were just as bad. I was in the thick of the crush and often I had no time to compose or even focus properly, but they were great situations which had to be recorded on film to get an insight into the band's life on tour.

"The book includes portraits which show the different characters in the band and the audiences who at times where more entertaining than the band. It was obvious how few punks there were outside of London . . . punk hadn't spread out of the capital by that time, and many of the kids knew only what they had read about the band in the papers. There are also some shots taken at their soundchecks and then there's the gigs themselves. There's not much you can say about them . . . the proof is here in the shots of the band in action giving their all. Last but not least there are some backstage shots. You can see that by the end of each gig the band was totally wrecked . . . John felt it the worst because of his non-stop energetic antics. They also invited some pretty bizarre people back into the dressing rooms.

"John was the leader of the band. Quick witted, humorous, arrogant, intelligent . . . he loved the attention, the fame, the glory. He was born for this and he knew he was a star. Although he wasn't the founder of the band (McLaren was), when he was on stage he took control, driving the audience into wild hysterics with his antics and sheer energy. Like a man possessed he would dance and prance and skank and groove and scream and shout . . . but it all made sense. He was doing exactly what the audience wanted to do themselves . . . like kids in an adventure playground.

"Offstage John was like a king holding court. He always had the right answers, always had the wit, and when he said another band or singer was shit, you believed they were shit because he said so. When on the road he was completely different from the others. While Sid found enjoyment in wrecking things, John would spend most of his time listening to music or drinking quietly. We used to spend hours together, talking and smoking and listening to reggae music. He had funny habits. At any spare moment you would find him asleep conserving energy or planning.

"The first thing he would do when he got back to the hotel or dressing room was to attack any spot he found on his face. Looking the part was important . . . the clothes were important. He began to realise the potential of what he was doing . . . what could be won or lost. His clothes began to change from heavy punk to chic punk, baggy trousers and crepe shoes. He would try outfits out in particular places. In Sweden it was baggy trousers . . . in certain parts of England it was the full works, leather and chains. He began to truly know himself and his abilities.

"When they got to America Sid's drug problem must have become too much and – as John said to me himself – never stay with a sinking ship.

"Sid was a strange person. He was brought into the band through John when Matlock was thrown out. He was a close friend of John's but in the end they became enemies. He was a regular punter at their early gigs and apparently he invented the pogo dance. Deep down he was a shy person . . . when on stage his reputation for notoriety didn't fit at all. I think he was frightened of the audiences because he became quite withdrawn on stage. Sometimes he showed no emotion at all.

"In the beginning he and John were great friends but somewhere along the line Sid found Nancy and drugs – heavy heavy drugs – which John wanted no part of. John would plead with him to get rid of her but to Sid she was like a crutch. When they were together he was like a kitten but without her he would go crazy. Often on tour he would wreck his room, take drugs, slash his body . . . anything that tempted him.

"All through the tour he was erratic. No one knew why. It seemed he missed Nancy. Sometimes he wouldn't eat at all. He'd drink heavy and take lots of drugs and even forget some of the songs. By the time they got to America it was all too much. John flew back to Britain half way through the tour. Sid stayed with Nancy. It was the end. The rest is history.

"Steve Jones saw his role in the band as the guitar hero and he played the part on and off stage. He was a great character, always seeing the funny side to every situation. At some of the gigs playing was virtually impossible and he had this habit of running into the audience and pulling faces. Off stage he and Paul Cook had the reputation of being ladies' men . . . chatting up anything in sight. Often they would have the most amazing parties behind closed doors in hotels. Shouts and screams of delight could be heard, and when the ladies came out of their rooms there was this look of satisfaction on every face. But behind this charade he was a great guitarist. He was a big part of that great Pistols' sound on record, driving every song to great heights.

"It wasn't until after the band split that I got to know Paul Cook. We used to see each other at gigs and he was a great admirer of my band Basement 5. While he was in the Pistols he appeared withdrawn, hardly ever communicating with John or Sid. He was closest to Steve and they would get up to all sorts of tricks together. He seemed more interested in playing than in anything else.

"I hope these pictures will make it clear what the period from 1975-1977 was like. Remember . . . punk is a state of mind not a way of dress."

Dennis Morris, 1991.

Soundcheck

When soundchecking the band found spare moments to laugh amongst themselves in between crafting their unique sound.

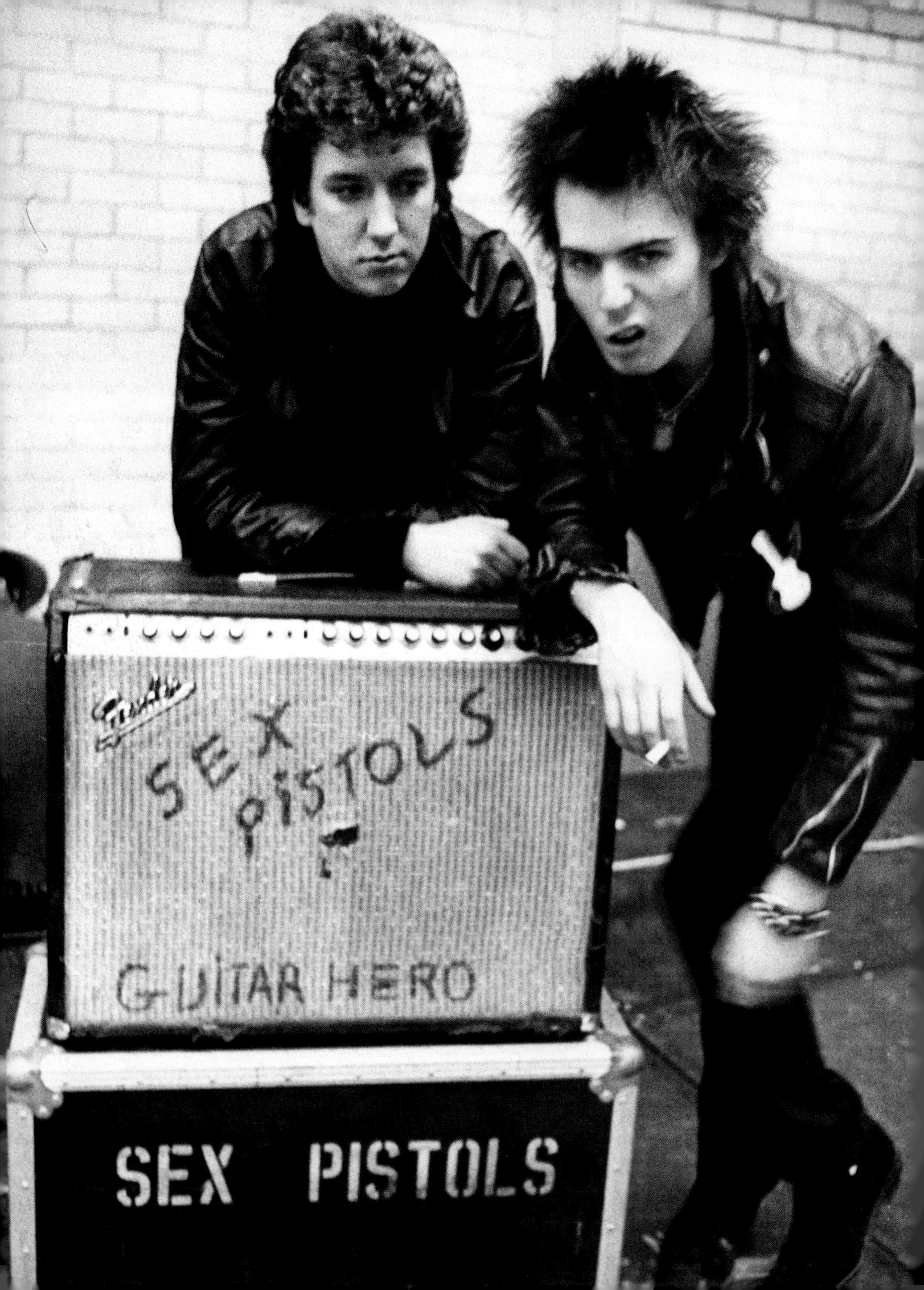
SEX PISTOLS
GUITAR HERO
SEX PISTOLS

The Punters

Sometimes the gigs were more about the audience, especially when the band played at some of the tiny clubs where there were no stage lights, nothing in fact to separate the band from the audience. At these gigs the crowd went wild, kicking, pushing and spitting. It was sheer hell. The only thing to do on these occasions was to concentrate on the crowds. They were the gigs on nights like these.

In Sweden the band played this tiny club. The only security was a rope three feet from the band. From the moment the band started playing this guy went berserk. It was as if some part of his brain had been triggered.

In Coventry the security barrier was human, four bouncers. It was the usual scene, club too small, too many punters — all hell broke loose.

Coventry.

Seconds later someone threw a bottle at the stage.

The gig was stopped. The security tried to restore some sort of order. The punters felt cheated, John kept winding them up, temperatures boiled – bang – a fight broke out.

John loved it.

The Gigs

When on stage the band created hysteria. The main instigator was John, skanking and prancing. Like a man possessed he would wind the punters up to a feverish pitch, followed by Steve Jones, guitar hero, with his classic stances. Sid was quite withdrawn, only occasionally reacting to the crowd. It was not until the American tour that his other side came out on stage. Paul Cook was the anchor man keeping the tight pounding beat. He held it all together. They were the most compulsive band to watch.

Pictures on succeeding pages from Brunel University, Penzance and London's Marquee Club.

Too much to drink, too much to smoke, club too hot, punters too demanding. Suddenly John threw up.

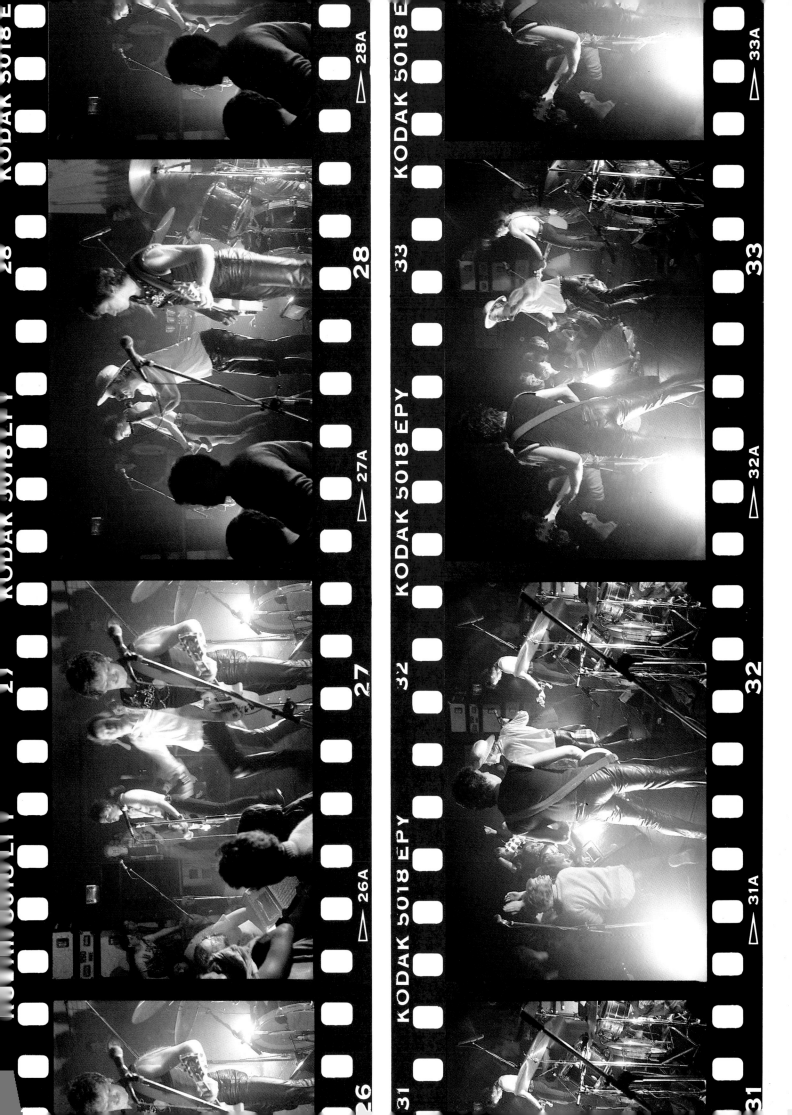

Portraits

Malcolm McLaren. The Instigator.

LOAD NOT TO
EXCEED 3750 LBS.
OR 25 PEOPLE

Johnny Rotten. The undisputed leader of the band. Backstage, Marquee Club.

Recording Pretty Vacant.

Sid lived up to the image of rock and roll. Sid Vicious, Sweden.

Sid's hotel room in Coventry after a night of drugs and booze.

Steve Jones, the guitar hero. The glamour boy of the band.

Paul Cook, the drummer. The quietest member of the band, closest to Steve Jones.

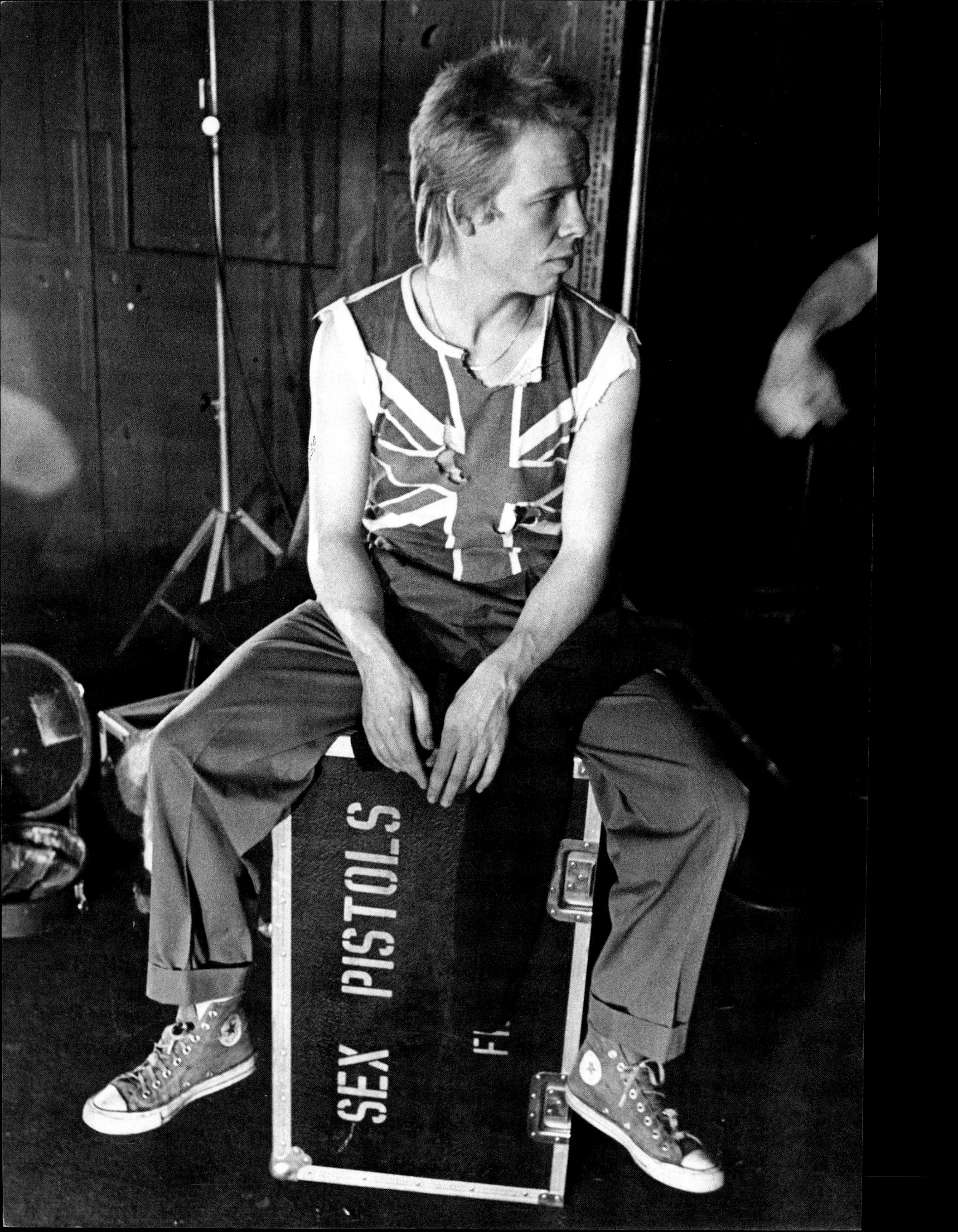
SEX PISTOLS

Paul Cook, Steve Jones and Rodent. Sweden.

Backstage

Not many people were allowed backstage, but those that were were pretty bizarre.

Some gigs were really painful, especially if the audience were too demanding.
Sometimes it took its toll on the band.

Sid and Nancy are backstage at Brunel University.

Steve Jones, punter and Sid Vicious. Backstage at Brunel University.

At the Penzance gig this guy appeared. He was a friend of John's and his name was Wobble. John called him Jah Wobble. I didn't know it then but that was the beginning of the end of The Sex Pistols and the beginning of PIL.

Special thanks to:
Susanna Frye for co-ordination
India Saffire Rose-Morris for inspiration.

© 1991 Dennis Morris Publications
This edition © 1991 Omnibus Press
(a division of Book Sales Limited.)

Book designed by Dennis Morris and Bob Aitken
Cover designed by Bob Aitken

ISBN 0.7119.2555.0
Order No. OP 46416

Exclusive distributors:

Book Sales Limited,
8/9 Frith Street, London W1V 5TZ, UK.

Music Sales Corporation,
225 Park Avenue South, New York, NY 10003, USA.

Music Sales Pty Limited,
120 Rothchild Avenue, Rosebery, NSW 2018, Australia.

To the Music Trade only:

Music Sales Limited,
8/9 Frith Street, London W1V 5TZ, UK.

Printed in England by: Ebenezer Baylis and Son Limited, Worcester